A Handbook for Christian Life in the 21st Century

Eric W. Gritsch

American Lutheran Publicity Bureau
Delhi, New York

The American Lutheran Publicity Bureau wishes to acknowledge
and thank Jeffery Neal Larson for the cover artwork, and
Martin A. Christiansen for his typesetting and production.

© American Lutheran Publicity Bureau
All rights reserved in the United States of America

American Lutheran Publicity Bureau
P.O. Box 327
Delhi, New York 13753
(607) 746-7511
www.alpb.org

ISBN 1-892921-06-5

Eric W. Gritsch, *A Handbook for Christian Life in the 21st Century*
(Delhi, NY: ALPB Books, 2005).

TABLE OF CONTENTS

Preface 3

Introduction 9

1. Evil 15

2. Justice 23

3. Baptism 31

4. Church 39

5. The Lord's Supper 47

6. Prayer 55

7. Music 61

Conclusion 69

References 71

"Be wise as serpents and innocent as doves."
(Matt. 10:16)

"He [God] will strengthen you to the end, so that you may be blameless on the day of our Lord Jesus Christ."
(1 Cor. 1:8)

"Let [Christians] never stop until they have proved by experience and are certain that they have taught the devil to death."
(Martin Luther, *Large Catechism*, Preface, 19)

Preface

What Buckminster Fuller (1895-1983) said about half a century ago has become even more apparent in the 21st century: "Spaceship earth" — fast, crowded and confusing — is in dire need of an instruction book, also a Christian one.[1] The world has become small and dangerous. Air traffic makes the major places in the world accessible within a day or two; computers bring minds together within minutes, regardless of distance. Love of neighbor, as well as hate of neighbor, can be globally headquartered. But any reality-check suggests that terrorists are more effective than pioneers of a universal citizenship for peace and justice. World religions are better known through their ineffective piety than through their power of love. Some religions have bred fanatic terrorism; others have created a confusing rhetoric of spirituality. Despite some periodic efforts of reform, Christianity remains stuck in a paralyzing struggle with a culture driven by ego-power. Its originally severe doctrine of sin has been compromised by an ecclesiastical arrogance of power that can hardly be distinguished from worldly politics. A noisy Christian right-wing has reduced Christian education to convenient slogans and superficial thinking.

> "The Bible guides every aspect of my life," boasts the Fundamentalist who flies airplanes and shops in supermarkets.
>
> "As a good Christian I never tell a lie," intones the politician.
>
> "Make your altar call now," urges the revival preacher, "or you will go straight to hell."

I have experienced such a world full of dangerous illusions, expressed in slogans and uniform thinking. The regime of Adolf Hitler made me a "Hitler Youth" at age ten (1941). I was taught to live and die for "one people, one country, one leader." When Hitler lost his war against the rest of the world, I was drafted into quickly organized army units to fight the massive Communist assault of Josef Stalin at the end of the Second World War (1945). I survived through desertion and adaptation to hard times, living in the Russian sector during the military occupation of Austria. Critical reflections about these experiences made me a theologian, shaped by Lutheranism and schooled at the universities in Vienna, Zürich, Basel and Yale. My so-called Confirmation in 1946 disclosed to me the poverty of catechetical instruction. I became convinced that the rite of Confirmation, if maintained at all, should not occur before age 16 (or when society declares a young person to be an "adult").

Other survivors, especially the psychiatrist Viktor Frankl (1905-1997) whose work was shaped by his holocaust experience as a young physician, taught me to live with the question of the meaning of a seemingly meaningless life. As a pastor and church historian, I tried to instruct candidates for the ordained ministry and others for more than three decades to combine sharp, critical academic work with spiritual formation for everyday life.

Ever since the first Christian generation spiritual "rules," "formulas," or "confessions" offered brief summaries of the faith to adults before their baptism, or to the young who had been baptized as infants and needed to "confirm" their baptism (usually between the ages of seven and fourteen). Biblical passages were used in the beginning (for example, Phil. 2:5-11, probably the oldest confession of Christ as Lord). When Christianity began to dominate culture in the fourth century, creeds became the core of instruction, such as the Apostles' Creed and the Nicene Creed of 325 C. E. The North African Bishop Augustine (354-430) called such instruction "catechism" (from the Latin *catechizare*, derived from the Greek *catechein*, "oral instruction"). This type of catechism became more elaborate in the Western church, the Roman Catholic Church, after the schism of 1054 C. E. which divided Roman Catholicism and Eastern Orthodoxy. The traditional catechism dealt with three topics: The Ten Commandments, the Apostles' Creed and the Lord's Prayer. Martin

Luther added two more topics, baptism and the Lord's Supper, based on the conviction that all baptized Christians constitute a "common priesthood" who needs training for their witness and service in the world.[2] He also used a question-and-answer method to overcome wide-spread illiteracy and to provide lessons learned by heart.

Other sixteenth-century educators, also known as "Humanists," such as Erasmus of Rotterdam (1469-1536) developed a "handbook," or "enchiridion" (from the Greek *encheiridion*, "something put into the hands," or a "dagger" for the Christian as a soldier fighting evil).[3] Luther called *The Small Catechism* a "handbook" and "enchiridion;"[4] he also knew hymnals as "enchiridia" because they provide instruction about the Christian faith and regulate worship.[5]

Other Protestant catechisms, such as *The Heidelberg Catechism* of 1563 and *The Westminster Confession* of 1646, explicate varying lists of topics, often concentrating on differences regarding the interpretation of the Lord's Supper and of the office of the ministry. Luther's *Large Catechism* has been modernized, for example, by Robert W. Jenson.[6] The Roman Catholic Church has continually updated and expanded its medieval catechism; the latest version is quite voluminous.[7]

Inherited traditional catechesis needs radical reform. Critical hindsight suggests rather obvious, persuasive reasons for a new model of spiritual formation.

1. Traditional handbooks/catechisms have become too old for an age in which traditional institutions no longer inspire confidence, especially in the family, government and the church. Catechesis relied on such institutions as the context for wholesome nurture, ranging from child-like trust to common sense for tackling the difficulties of life in a complex world.

2. Much pedagogical non-sense, indeed esoteric doctrine, appear under the buzz-word "spirituality." Instead of describing Christian life guided by the Holy Spirit, it has become an intellectual curtain, as it were, hiding a theological illiteracy and a spiritual bankruptcy. Struggling for institutional survival, denominational head-

quarters grind out exercises grounded in such a superficial spirituality and modeled after popular self-help guides promising a successful diet for mind and body.

3. Congregations suffer from an imbalance between worship and education. Word and sacraments are celebrated in a variety of ways, but minds are not challenged to create a style of life that moves from Sunday worship to Monday living with "spiritual formation" (a designation indicating the combination of worship and education to create an effective Christian style of life).

I see such critical hindsight crystallized in two principal reasons for the increasing decay of the catechetical enterprise. Both reasons are interrelated and also constitute the core of spiritual formation for everyday life: 1) *An underestimation of evil*, and 2) *A lack of joy in everyday life*. For only when the deceiving forces of evil are faced in everyday life with the power of faith in a never-ending future with God through Christ is it possible to experience genuine joy in everyday life. That is why this handbook begins with a diagnosis or reality-check of evil and ends with music as the essential ingredient of joyful celebration.

Martin Luther (1483-1546) was the pioneer of post-medieval catechesis. His diagnosis of the sixteenth-century catechetical enterprise in the congregations of the Saxon country-side also describes situations in parishes today:

> Dear God, what misery I beheld! The ordinary person knows absolutely nothing about the Christian faith, and unfortunately many pastors are completely unskilled and incompetent teachers. Yet supposedly they all bear the name Christian, are baptized and receive the holy sacrament, even though they do not know the Lord's Prayer, the Creed, or the Ten Commandments. As a result they live like simple cattle or irrational pigs and, despite the fact that the gospel has been returned, have mastered the fine art of misusing all their freedom.[8]

Acknowledgements

Numerous individuals from all walks of life, survivors of vari-ous sorts, Sunday School teachers, pastors and ecumenists from various denominations have shared with me their negative experiences with existing handbooks or catechisms and have encouraged me to provide something "modern." I tested and improved this handbook at the Melanchthon Institute in Houston, TX, where I have a teaching chair. I also involved a number of Lutheran pastors and their congregations, especially the Rev. Dr. Robert Moore, Christ the King Lutheran Church, Houston, TX; Pastor Lawrence R. Recla who tested the handbook with the Queens location of the Diakonia Program of the New York Metropolitan Synod of the Evangelical Lutheran Church in America (ELCA); the New York Chapter of Lutheran pastors in the Society of the Holy Trinity; the ELCA Conference of Pastors in Indianapolis, IN; the Adult Forum of my own church, Zion Church of the City of Baltimore (ELCA); Pastor Kirsten Drigsdahl and her colleagues in the Lutheran diocese of Helsingore, Denmark; and interested friends from various walks of life in Europe and in the United States. Samuel Brown, a specialist in electrical and computer engineering who is also a musician, helped me find appropriate samples of modern Christian music and made other helpful suggestions. The lyrics from "Mineral" are cited with permission from "Crank!" A Record Company, 1223 Wilshire Boulevard #823, Santa Monica, CA 90403. Norman A. Hjelm, a good friend and an experienced editor, did a critical reading which helped to shape the final draft. Martin A. Christiansen did the layout/design for printing. Randy Chase Yoder produced the photograph of the author. Jeffrey Neal Larson created the cover illustration. My spouse, Bonnie, an expert teacher in Sunday and Monday schools, has given me professional advice, especially in the drafting of pedagogical questions at the end of each segment. As the spouse of a "theologian of the cross" and as a teacher of juvenile delinquents she, too, knows the gallows humor that helped me and some of her students to survive in the face of tremendous odds.

Finally, I thank the American Lutheran Publicity Bureau, especially its Executive Director, the Rev. Dr. Frederick J. Schumacher, for publishing this handbook. It reflects the spirit of Luther's insight and contention that his reform movement did not intend to create a new denomination but to heal the ills of the church *and* of the world — also in the 21st century.

— Eric W. Gritsch

Introduction

This *Handbook* amplifies traditional catechesis by offering a pattern of spiritual formation for everyday life in the 21st century. It instructs baptized Christians as people who, according to the ancient Christian tradition, live as pilgrims between Christ's first and second advent. They are people on "the Way" (Acts 24:14) to a future "where righteousness is at home" (2 Peter 3:13). They are "strangers and foreigners on earth" (Hebr. 11:13), and they are "ambassadors for Christ" in a strange land (2 Cor. 5:20). Pilgrim people travel with few comforts, face unforeseen obstacles and remain alert in order to stay on track. They are continually confronted by evil which cannot be fully measured or explained. Thus they must become *"wise as serpents and innocent as doves,"* otherwise they will be like "sheep in the midst of wolves" (Matt. 10:16). This is Jesus' mandate for mission, combined with his general commandment to "make disciples of all nations" through baptism (Matt. 28:19).

The four types of animals describe the experience of mission entrusted to the disciples. If they behave just like sheep, belonging to an unguarded and naïve flock, they will be devoured by wolves. "Brother will betray brother to death, and a father his child, and children will rise against parents and have them put to death; and you will be hated by all because of my name" (Matt. 10:21-22). If they behave like doves, cooing with love and joy on the roof-tops, they represent a child-like faith often manifested in the public use of spiritual gifts, such as speaking in tongues. But in a hostile environment they will quickly die because they are easy targets for hunters (who know that most fowl can be shot at close range when they make love). Jesus called for disciples who combine the gift of the Holy Spirit (symbolized by the dove) with cold-blooded wisdom (symbolized by the serpent).

The image of the *serpent* has an interesting history in the Bible. First, the serpent is the instrument of temptation in the garden, promising Adam and Eve that they "will not die" and that they "will be like God" (Gen. 3:5) when they follow their own desires and eat the forbidden fruit from the tree "in the middle of the garden." Then, the serpent becomes a symbol of salvation from death during the Exodus of the people of Israel from Egypt. Moses was told by God to make a bronze serpent, and anyone who was bitten by a poisonous serpent survived by looking at the bronze serpent (Num. 21:9). Finally, when Jesus met the Jewish leader Nicodemus at night for a discussion of how to be born again, he was told by Jesus, "Just as Moses lifted up the serpent in the wilderness, so must the Son of Man be lifted up, that whoever believes in him shall not perish but may have eternal life" (John 3:14). So the serpent becomes a symbol of healing and salvation, an image also shared by ancient Greeks as well as modern medicine. The serpent appears as a logo for medicine, curled around a staff. But healing and salvation do not occur without a precise, correct and cold-blooded diagnosis of an illness. *To be wise as a serpent means to use the mind for a proper diagnosis in order to move to a proper prognosis and treatment for survival.*

This *Handbook* is a survival kit, as it were, based on a careful, rational examination of everyday life. "*Serpenthood*" is the key to effective Christian education and spiritual formation for survival. It is the counterpart to "dovehood" when Christians, like "innocent doves" (Matt. 10:16) praise God in child-like faith and give thanks for salvation from evil, sin and death through Christ. But the dialectic of serpentine wisdom and dove-like faith has been neglected in Christian spiritual formation. Christian history is filled with the work of the mind to reach "beyond nature" (from the Latin *super naturam*), or go "behind nature" (from the Greek *meta physis*). Supernaturalism and metaphysics produced tomes of scholastic and moral theology offering a gymnastics of rationalism ranging from proofs for the existence of God to sophisticated arguments of how God as the severe judge of sin may be appeased by "good works." But since God has offered salvation from sin not through wrath but through love in Christ alone, by grace alone and by faith alone, any rational penetration of this divine mystery is off limits. This insight of faith does not call for a Christian anti-intellectualism, the sacrifice of the mind for faith. On the contrary, this divine mystery liberates the human mind from the temptation of metaphysical or supernatural speculations about salvation for a total concentration on the spiritual formation of faith active in love in the world. Consequently, the chief work of the Christian mind is the diagnosis of evil as the first step in developing a style of life geared to realistic witness in word and deed. Christian ethics, therefore, is not obedience to numerous unchanging commandments of God, as listed in the Bible or constructed in the post-biblical tradition. What was once labeled "evil" may later become "good" and vice-versa.

The German pastor and theologian Dietrich Bonhoeffer (1906-1945), who joined the military conspiracy to assassinate Adolf Hitler, argued for a radical difference between traditional ethical reflection and Christian ethics:

> The knowledge of good and evil seems to be the aim of ethical reflection. The first task of Christian ethics is to invalidate this knowledge. Neither the "struggle for one's rights" nor the "renunciation of one's rights" is anything in itself, or can itself be, for example, a topic of the Church's proclamation, but in faith both are submission to the right which belongs only to God. Consequently, there are not two scales of values, one for the world and one for the Christians, but there is the one and only word of God which demands faith and obedience.[9]

Faith is the basis of an ethics of obedience which uses the power of reason to diagnose evil and to discover the best possible ways to extend the love of God in Christ to all areas of life.

During the mean mean-time between Christ's first and second coming there must also be scheduled occasions for the pilgrim people of God to gather for worship and education. *A Hymnal provides order for worship. A Handbook teaches Christians how to live and to die, to laugh and to cry.* It should be used with diligence, passion, indeed with a gallows humor.

> Those who go out weeping, bearing the seed for sowing, shall come home with shouts of joy (Ps. 126:6).
>
> Blessed are you who weep now, for you will laugh (Luke 6:21).

"Serpenthood" has been overshadowed by *"servanthood"* in the long tradition of Christian humility based on faith, love and service.

> The greatest among you will be your servant. All who exalt themselves will be humbled, and all who humble themselves will be exalted (Matt. 23:11-12).

But humility has too often underestimated evil, indeed was penetrated by it. Tough and courageous monastic groups, both monks and nuns, have been weakened, indeed became ineffective, when they succumbed to admiration from the outside and zealous piety inside. The humility of ecclesiastical offices disappeared in a context of power, pomp and circumstance. There is always the temptation of becoming proud of one's humility; or anxious over the lack of it, thus creating a life without joy. Effective Christian servants must be on the alert against the lures of evil. *Servanthood must be combined with Serpenthood.* For only when Christians have encountered evil, diagnosed and contained it through forms of justice, will they be able to do effective service and experience genuine joy. *That is why this handbook teaches the move from servanthood to a dialectic of serpenthood and dovehood.* Such a move creates the foundation for an effective spiritual formation for everyday life in the 21st century.

This spiritual formation could be described in many ways, considering the long and varied history of Christian education and worship. I have selected the absolute minimum of seven components of spiritual formation as the quintessential, ecumenically grounded stages whose pedagogical progression creates the spiritual athletics, as it were, for the Christian run through life in the mean (and often mean!) time between Christ's first and second advent.

> Athletes exercise self-control in all things; they do it to receive a perishable wreath, but we an imperishable one. So I do not run aimlessly, nor do I box as though beating the air, but I punish my body and enslave it so that after proclaiming to others I myself should not be disqualified (1 Cor. 9:25-27).

This handbook offers seven components of contemporary spiritual formation: 1) Evil, 2) justice, 3) baptism, 4) the church, 5) the Lord's Supper, 6) prayer and 7) music.

Evil and *justice* are realities encountered by all human beings, regardless of religion or any belief in God. When Christianity dominated and controlled everyday life, every aspect of reality was piously viewed as Christian or pagan. A domineering ecclesiastical optimism crept into the medieval church as "the institution of salvation," confident in its power to exorcise evil from its dominant place in life. The church simply identified evil with anyone and anything in opposition to its doctrine and morality. Critical inquiry into established doctrine and diversity in behavior were identified as marks of evil, and justice meant to eradicate them as victims of the power of Satan, at home in favorite scapegoats, such as witches, heretics and social outcasts in general. When society was "secularized" or "de-churched," the diagnosis of evil became much more complicated. But in the distant past as well as in the present the encounter with evil and the need for justice are part of everyday life. This two-fold experience is the environment of Christian catechesis which usually begins with baptism.

This environment has been underestimated, indeed neglected, by an unrealistic Christian view of the world as less polluted by evil than it is. Just a few moments with televised global communication of "bad news" will make it obvious how powerful evil is and why justice is needed. *To omit the treatment of evil from Christian instruction would be the same as omitting reading and writing from elementary education.* That is why spiritual formation must begin with a consideration of *evil* and *justice* as the powerful context of the Christian life beginning with *baptism*. It initiates into a community, *the church*, where Christ is most visibly present in the *Lord's Supper*. *Prayer* is the way to communicate with God about anything, at any time and in any place; and *music* is the most universal way to express praise and thanksgiving as well as suffering and longing for a better life.

Each topic of the *Handbook* is treated in three ways, inviting serpentine discussion and decisions regarding spiritual formation. The indented text portions offer biblical and other sources as well as practical examples. All biblical quotations are from the *New Revised Standard Version of the Holy Bible*. All other sources are listed under numbered "References."

This Handbook has only one pedagogical prerequisite: Curious minds who wonder about everyday life and search for meaning, indeed have sensed the phenomenon of survival. Any group of any size from all walks of life, or from any Christian denomination, is invited to use this *Handbook*. It invites Christians and non-Christians to assess the experience of evil and the need for justice as essential parts of human existence. Salvation from evil, sin and death through faith in Jesus Christ is offered to anyone in the world. This distinction between the struggle for justice (*law*) and the promise of a never-ending life with God through Christ (*gospel*) puts the stamp *Lutheran* on this handbook. Lutheranism began as a reform movement within the Western church for the preservation and nurture of the essential teachings of the church catholic.[10] The task of reform continues, and thus a Lutheran handbook is simultaneously an ecumenical handbook. Its instruction is offered to all Christians.

Questions are listed after each chapter to initiate discussion on each topic. Participants should also share their own experiences regarding the seven stages of spiritual formation. There should be ample time for discussion, indeed argumentation, about each of the seven catechetical topics. Participants may engage a qualified teacher; or, after they have collected and organized their findings, they may use a theological specialist to refine their learning. But the teacher and/or specialist should be a resource person rather than a traditional teacher of a class. He/she should share his/her expertise in patient, yet disciplined dialogue with all participants. In this sense, the handbook should create a partnership of learning and should achieve its two basic objectives: 1) *The best possible diagnosis of reality encountered in everyday life — a reality check through the exercise of serpenthood, and 2) an integration of the seven topics in such a way that they become the foundation for a spiritual formation linked to celebration — the experience of joy in the exercise of dovehood.* "Graduation exercises" could consist of individual and group definitions of the seven topics. The topics should become guiding principles in personal and group experiences of everyday life, especially in congregations as the most concrete expressions of the church catholic. There could also be a concluding musical celebration through singing, performing, or just listening.

I
Evil

This handbook begins with the question of evil because evil, like death, is an undeniable reality in everyday life; something will always go wrong without rhyme or reason ("Murphy's Law").[11] Consequently, evil is like an unsolvable riddle or an unknown illness. The mystery of evil can be attractive like a first date; it can be like the accidental ingestion of poison which paralyzes mind and body; or it can create various dimensions of fear, ranging from senseless attempts to escape, or fanatic terrorism. Like a deadly disease, evil has symptoms, and their diagnosis in everyday life is the beginning of Christian education, or the first step of spiritual formation. The prevailing symptoms are: 1) *confusion*, 2) the temptation of *playing God* and 3) the lack of *enduring vigilance.*

Confusion

The designation "evil" has its roots in the word "diabolical" (from the Greek *diaballein* — "to set things apart by throwing them," "to confuse"). Evil creates confusion, elaborated into distraction, illusion, deception, fear and terror. It can be both attractive or ugly, representing a false security or sheer violence. Evil may be compared to a clever motion picture which creates artificial realities, thus luring its audience into illusions of comfort, or instilling fear through threatening illusions. Even documentary films may create a flight from reality, or instill fear. The reality of life outside the theater is cleverly veiled by an optical illusion on a screen in a dark space. There is a powerful drive of the human mind to deal with the vicissitudes of earthly life by trying to ignore them, or flee from them. Each generation has tried to veil the unpleasant problems of life by many means which, like drugs or gambling, lead to addiction — another popular symptom of evil.

In the Bible, evil is often portrayed as mental confusion, indeed as possession by an "evil spirit." There are countless evil spirits. When Jesus asked the Gerasene demoniac, "What is your name?," he replied, "My name is legion; for we are many" (Mark 5:9). One can list various descriptions, experiences and opinions about evil, or the devil and other popular notions of things or events which confuse, get out of control and endanger life. Every age has a favorite way of dealing with the power of confusion. In a political tyranny, often disguised as "people's democracy," confusion is seen manifested in diversity, as the enemy of uniformity. When Christians refused to worship the Roman emperor, they were viewed as evil because of their exclusive worship of the God of the Bible. Consequently, they were persecuted and killed. When Christianity became the religion of the empire by decree in the fourth century, curious Christian minds were pointed out as heretics or enemies of the state for their deviation from established doctrine and morality. There is the famous example of Galileo Gallilei (1564-1642) who denied the prevalent view of the sun rotating around the earth and was forced to recant his view of a sun-centered universe. Others, like John Hus (c. 1369-1415), were martyred for opposing the view of a divinely instituted papacy as the highest ecclesiastical authority in the medieval church.

Our time has become quite tolerant. As a result, individual or communal rights often clash, indeed become abusive. Citizens, for example may, vote for specific laws regarding the protection of private property; but when called into court for a violation they no longer abide by the laws they voted for but prefer the use of a gun to legal arbitration. A bumper sticker put it succinctly: "Shoot first, then talk." That is why our age encounters the danger of international terrorism, often in the guise of religion. What was once labeled "evil" may later become "good" and vice-versa. Thus confusion reigns. Indeed, sophisticated analysis often leads to paralysis, a state of enduring confusion in a life of fear and trembling.

Evil may be related to disease as a puzzling confusion between its theological interpretation as a "wage" of sin and its medical view as part of the forces of death.

> And the Lord God took the man [Adam] and put him in the garden of Eden to till it and keep it. And the Lord God commanded the man, "You shall freely eat of every tree of the garden; but of the tree of the knowledge of good and evil you shall not eat, for in the day that you eat of it you shall die" (Gen. 2:15-17).
>
> For the wages of sin is death (Rom. 6:23).

When disease cannot be diagnosed, it is feared in its mystery. But disease can also be caused by the evils of abuse of food, of drugs, or other temptations which make people sick and indeed cause them to die. The Bible affirms the power of faith over disease and death.

> When Jesus saw the faith of the people who brought a paralyzed man to him, he removed the disease and the man walked home (Matt. 8:2-7).
>
> Peter healed a crippled beggar (Acts 3:1-8).

Modern medicine is paying increased attention to the relationship between child-like faith and scientific ways to cure diseases. In this sense, confusion about diseases may be reduced by combined methods of scientific and spiritual diagnoses and treatments.

Playing God

The Bible diagnoses evil as idolatry — the rejection of the First of the Ten Commandments: "You shall have no other gods besides me" (Exod. 20:3). The "original sin" of humanity is the yielding to the temptation of playing God.

> God said, "You shall not eat of the fruit of the tree that is in the middle of the garden, nor shall you touch it, or you shall die." But the serpent said to the woman, "You will not die; for God knows that when you eat of it your eyes will be opened, and *you will be like God*, knowing good and evil" (Gen. 3:3-5).

> [They ate the forbidden fruit]. Then the eyes of both were opened and they knew that they were naked; and they sewed fig leaves together and made loincloths for themselves (Gen. 3:7).

Great expectations, but only self-deception!

The diagnosis of evil as playing God is a theological one, based on the insight of biblical faith in a God who created the world. Jews and Christians are given this insight as a disclosure of the basic rule that God is in charge of the world. But human creatures are tempted to take God's place. This is the real mystery of evil. Rational speculation about it leads nowhere. Did God permit evil by tempting Adam and Eve? Why could they not be satisfied with eating all the fruit from the many trees earmarked for them? Does God allow a fallen angel, Satan, or a clever serpent to create a hunger for absolute power? The human mind ends up in a circle of irrationality: the assumption of a God who allows a violation of divine law in order to punish human creatures, or, as the Christian biblical tradition suggests, to save them from punishment through the mediation of a Christ.

Playing God is the dangerous pastime of humankind after the violation of the commandment of letting God be God. To be in charge, to have total control over others and to enjoy such ego-power is the most common manifestation of evil in the world. Ego-power ranges from capricious claims ("Me-ism" — "What you have belongs to me") to murder and deception. Evil bears the mark of Cain who kills his brother Abel and lies about it.

> Cain said to his brother Abel, "Let us go out into the field." And when they were in the field, Cain rose up against his brother Abel and killed him. Then the Lord said to Cain, "Where is your brother Abel?" He said, "I do not know; am I my brother's keeper?" (Gen. 4:8-9).

Murder and deception are the worst symptoms of tyrants. Tyrants and tyrannies have existed in every age. They often begin their rule by promises of a better life through strength, impressing unsuspecting minds with their power.

Adolf Hitler offered jobs for the victims of bankruptcy in the 1930s. Hordes of young men were employed for low wages to build new highways (the *Autobahn*); and every German was promised a low-priced "people's car" (*Volkswagen*) to drive on the new roads. When Hitler had established his tyranny the highways belonged to the new political elite with their black limousines, and the Volkswagen became the German jeep in Hitler's battlefields.

There are always people who tell other people what to do; and there are always people who like to be told what to do. This is the birth of fascism in politics, or whatever form such power play takes. Children, parents, politicians, religious leaders strive for such power; the world has never been without it. "Playing God," idolatry, ranges from the terror of tyrants and terrorists to the seduction of reality into illusion. The enduring challenge of spiritual formation is the unmasking of evil through reality checks, and the sharing of the analyzed results with those who are unable or unwilling to face evil as the inevitable reality of everyday life.

Example: A teacher was unable to teach because of fear. He consulted a psychiatrist who, after a lengthy analysis, offered the diagnosis, "You have an inferiority complex that paralyses you in the classroom. Find another occupation." The teacher was advised by a good friend to get another expert opinion. So he went to another psychiatrist who, after a lengthy analysis, offered the diagnosis, "You do not have an inferiority complex. *You are inferior.*" Now the teacher could teach again, though not as well as many others, but well enough to make a living. He was weak, but not paralyzed. One could say with Paul, by way of analogy, that whenever one suffers for the sake of Christ, one is strong in weakness (2 Cor. 12:10).

Like in medicine, precise diagnosis based on findings and symptoms is the key to counter evil; only a thorough reality check will disclose the chances of surviving evil and containing its awesome power.

Enduring Vigilance

God-talk, theology, must begin by distinguishing what is disclosed by God and what is hidden. One can only discover the power of evil, but one cannot show why it exists. The answer to that question is not revealed by God. Theology begins with the notion of faith that evil can only be overcome by God through a Savior called "Jesus Christ." Because liberation from evil comes through faith in Christ alone, the human mind can be disciplined to stay focused on the evils in the world and thus avoid speculations about the origins of good and evil, or of God. For God is only known through human communication. Theology can only deal with what God has revealed, not with the hidden, unrevealed God.

> If I wish to know someone, I do so by asking for some self-disclosure, simultaneously sharing information about myself. Without such information I am tempted to make up the other person. Similarly, God is known through divine self-revelation, not through human speculation which makes up a view of God.
>
> Luther was once asked, "Where was God before the creation of the world?" He answered: "Yes, Augustine [354-430] mentioned this. But once when he was asked, he said, "God was making hell for those who are inquisitive."[12]

The mind is free from speculations about God and can concentrate on the problems of everyday life, making serpentine distinctions between various ways in which evil works. Without sharp discernment, indeed debate, evil is not realistically diagnosed. "Eternal vigilance is the price of liberty" (Thomas Jefferson).[13]

Christians need to become the people who, like the police, often exhibit their duty in the slogan seen on police cars, "to protect and to serve." They are to be like "911" operators, as it were, indeed be the 911 system for help against evil. They can be on call in order to save others from sudden terror or clever illusions. As people of

God on the pilgrimage to a better future, Christians, like the police or any other trained force on alert against evil, can use the insights gained from spiritual formation as an early warning system for others who do not have such advanced insights. Christian minds must stand enduring guard against evil. "An idle mind is the devil's workshop."[14] Not every Christian may be able to police evil in everyday life. Some must volunteer, or be drafted, to engage in special operations against evil. But no one is too weak to oppose evil once their commitment to Christ has become a spiritual reality.

> For we do not have a high priest who is unable to sympathize with our weaknesses, but we have one who in every respect has been tested as we are, yet without sin. Let us therefore approach the throne of grace with boldness, so that we may receive mercy and find grace to help in time of need (Hebr. 4:15-16).

Vigilance is the state of mind that concentrates on the unmasking of evil rather than on the unrevealed God. Once evil is diagnosed in its various manifestations, ways and means must be found to keep it from taking over. It is a matter of rational discipline which must discover that the struggle for survival is the enduring vigilance of letting God be God.

HAVE YOU THOUGHT ABOUT...

1. How would you describe evil in today's world?
2. Identify a time in your life when you were confronted by evil?
3. What are some strategies that you use to battle evil?
4. Identify ways in which evil may be described as illusive and/or deceiving?
5. When have you found yourself personifying evil? (For example talking about the devil or demons).

II
Justice

Once evil is diagnosed in specific ways it must be treated by being restrained enough to prevent chaos and confusion. Diagnosis leads to treatment even if there is no prognosis for removing evil in the world. This is done through laws which try to establish the best possible balance between chaos and order. This balance is based on what is commonly known as "the Golden Rule" or "the Ethics of Reciprocity," summarized in the saying, "Treat others as you would wish to be treated" — a way of mutual agreement that creates enough balance between good and evil to stem the tide of chaos. Lawlessness is chaos. The Golden Rule exists, in one form or another, in all major religions and cultures.

> In the Bible it is the double commandment, "You shall love the Lord your God with all your heart, and with all your soul, and with all your mind. This is the greatest and first commandment. And a second is like it, You shall love your neighbor as yourself" (Matt. 22:37-39).

Such rules are to create "justice," symbolized by a scale showing the balance between good and evil. But any reality check discovers that evil is always heavier than the good — a sign that evil may be prevented from exercising its full power, but will never let the good prevail. Justice is a fragile condition in the world. It is 1) *a wedge against backsliding*, 2) the basis of *cooperation for survival* and 3) it is *bonded with the righteousness of faith*.

A Wedge Against Backsliding

Although the Golden Rule demands an even balance between self-love and love of neighbor, no such balance is achieved by any individual or group. Even such a tough Christian as St. Paul loses his battle against injustice.

> I do not understand my own actions. For I do not do what I want, but I do the things I hate. Now if I do what I do not want, I agree that the law is good. But in fact it is no longer I that do it, but sin that dwells in me. For I know that nothing good dwells in me, that is in my flesh. I can will what is right, but I cannot do it. For I do not do the good I want, but the evil I do not want to do is what I do (Rom. 7:15-19).

Every saint has remained a sinner; no one has had a perfect record of righteousness. Generations of revival preachers have scolded crowds of guilt-ridden Christians for their back-sliding. The only marginal attainment of justice is the avoidance of massive global, tyranny, though tyrants always find their victims of fear. "Fear" is the worst four-letter word. "We have nothing to fear but fear itself" (Franklin D. Roosevelt).[15] Biblical heroes like David, Solomon, Job, Peter and Paul were made saints by pious ecclesiastical hind-sight, be it through popular adoration or formal canonization. In reality, they were problematic figures who had to be radically changed or "converted" in order to make it into the "good book."

> David committed adultery with Bathsheba and had her husband Uriah killed (2 Sam. 11).
>
> Solomon violated divine laws by living with hundreds of pagan women (1 Kings 11).
>
> Job was a pessimist who cursed the day he was born (Job 3).
>
> Peter was not the "rock" of faith (Matt. 16:18) and betrayed Jesus (Matt. 27:69-75).
>
> Paul was often confused and in doubt (Rom. 7:14-20).

To love others as much as one loves oneself remains an ideal. The best attempts to balance the scale between justice and injustice may be efforts of moral tithing, doing ten percent "good works," but they are exceptions rather than the rule.

Cooperation for Survival
Anyone, regardless of religion and culture, can work with others to avoid chaos. It is like the four-way stop sign at an intersection: drivers agree to stop at their corner before proceeding further; and so offer the other drivers a chance to cross safely. It is an agreement to obey traffic laws for safe driving. Such and similar laws (like "exit" signs in crowded rooms) have no religious significance and little, if any, moral weight. Drivers at intersections do not intend to become friends; one or two may wave their hands as a polite gesture of patience. The laws just provide mutual protection and save from injury or death.

> Someone is drowning and is pulled out of the water by three swimmers: a Christian, a Communist and a Hindu. They proudly proclaim that their religious convictions motivated their good deed. The action was the same, though the confession of faith made it a Christian, a Communist and a Hindustani deed. "It makes no difference *who* saved me," said the survivor. "I just wanted to be pulled from the water."

To balance life and death, poverty and wealth, education and ignorance, or whatever two unequal sides are present, is a common task for the sake of survival. Civilized life requires cooperation by law and order; it rejects the ethics of survival of the fittest. Justice is a wedge against crude selfishness, against idolatry, playing God. The constant work for balance by laws is the best way to treat and contain evil before it becomes sheer terror without any agreed-upon laws. "Injustice anywhere is a threat to justice everywhere" (Martin Luther King, Jr.).[16]

Bonded With the Righteousness of Faith
Worldly justice should be linked to Christian righteousness. Christians join non-Christians in the effort to create justice as a way to curb the fury of evil and to assure protection through a balance of

power. But Christians become right with God and just in God's sight because they are made "righteous" by faith in Jesus Christ who stood in for them when they were subject to punishment for their idolatry.

> For our sake he made him to be sin who knew no sin, so that in him we might become the righteousness of God (2 Cor.5:21).

> He [Jesus] gave himself for our sins to set us free from the present evil age (Gal. 1:4).

The "original sin" in the garden has forfeited any opportunity to be accepted by God through one's own efforts. Human minds have tried in vain to argue for a way to make good for that "fall" from the original, sinless relationship between human creatures and God. But neither the argument for a "free will" to decide for or against salvation (who would decide against it?), nor the notion of some kind of cooperation between good intentions and God's grace have held water. Any critical reality check shows that such efforts are figments of imagination: how can I choose to be saved or damned when I cannot even choose when to be born, when to remain healthy or sick, or how long to live? If I think I can intend to choose my own destiny I only discover the truth of the old adage, "The road to hell is paved with good intention." Moreover, the idealistic notion of earning righteousness before God has little if any effective consequences for a better life on earth. Even faith in Jesus Christ is never so strong as to create a better world. This is the experience of Christian life in the interim between Christ's first and second coming.

> In accordance with his [God's] promise, we wait for new heavens and a new earth, where righteousness is at home (2 Peter 3:13).

> So if anyone is in Christ, there is a new creation: everything old has passed away; see, everything has become new! (2 Cor. 5:17).

Earthly justice is a rational compromise for survival through a minimal balance of law and order. This compromise never reconciles one person with another, or creates good will and peace on earth. It simply prevents the worst. The four-way stop sign at an intersection does not make friends; it only prevents the senseless behavior of those without any regard for their neighbor.

Righteousness with God can only be achieved through the God who mysteriously becomes "the Son of God", the Savior from evil through his own death as the way for all human sinners to join a new creation without evil. It is the Christmas gift of faith through the baby Jesus on the way to Good Friday and Easter. No mind can comprehend how the divine incarnation in Jesus is done. There is only room for wonder and adoration.

> I wonder as I wander under the sky,
> how Jesus the Savior did
> come to die for poor ordinary people
> like you and like I.[17]
>
> Joy to the world, the Lord is come!
> Let earth receive its king.
> Let ev'ry heart prepare him room,
> and heaven and nature sing.[18]

Here serpentine reason is joined by dove-like faith. The task of earthly justice gives way to sheer joy about a unique gift that cannot be earned: the love of God in Christ for disobedient creatures who become righteous by faith in Christ alone.

The mind can only try to create ways of containing the worst of evil through law and order. Justice is the result of the work of the mind struggling with evil; righteousness is the gift of the Holy Spirit anticipating victory over evil.

> Let each of you not look to your own interests, but to the interests of others. Let the same mind be in you that was in Christ Jesus who, though he was in the form of God, did not regard equality with God as something to be exploited, but emptied himself, taking the form of a slave, being born in human likeness. And being found in human

form, he humbled himself and became obedient to the point of death — even the death on a cross (Phil. 2:4-8).

Human laws, aiming for survival from the power of evil, create some justice, but never its full measure, a proper balance between good and evil. Thus justice only reveals how powerful evil is. "For through the law comes the knowledge of sin" (Rom. 3:20). To work for justice is the frustrating task of policing the world to avoid total chaos and terror. Only the righteousness of faith creates the liberating joy of knowing about a future without evil.

> For now we see in a mirror dimly, but then we will see face to face. Now I know only in part; then I will know fully, even as I have been fully known (1 Cor. 13:12).

Earthly justice and spiritual righteousness are intertwined in the Christian life. The realm of the law, with its bad news about the lasting power of evil, is mixed with the realm of the gospel, with its good news about Christ's victory over evil. While serpentine wisdom winds its way through an evil world, it is warmed by the bright sun of dove-like faith on the trek to a future world without evil. Life in the two realms of the good faith and the evil forces in the world is a tough yet confident struggle.

> When we stress that faith ought to be certain and secure we do not have in mind a certainty without doubt, or a security without anxiety. Rather, we affirm that believers have a perpetual struggle with their own lack of faith, and are far from possessing a peaceful conscience, never interrupted by any disturbance. On the other hand, we want to deny that they may fall out of, or depart from, their confidence in the divine mercy, no matter how much they may be troubled (John Calvin, 1509-1564).[19]

Christians can cooperate with any other group for justice by diagnosing evil in its particular appearance at specific times and places. When evil is embodied in tyranny, justice may only be achieved by sharp-minded, cold-blooded resistance. Minimal justice consists in free speech and respect for law and order based on individual rights. But like in the case of deadly cancer, early detection and diagnosis are essential for survival.

> When Adolf Hitler established his tyranny in Germany, he was opposed by the naval hero of World War I, Martin Niemoeller (1892-1984) who had become a pacifist pastor. When a student asked him, "How could this happen?," he replied: "First, they came for the Communists, but I was not a Communist; so I did not speak out. Then they came for the Socialists and the Trade Unionists, but I was neither, so I did not speak out. Then they came for the Jews, but I was not a Jew; so I did not speak out. And when they came for me, there was no one left to speak out for me."[20]

While others may maintain some optimism about everyday life — "things are never as bad as they seem;" "I can do just about everything if I desire to do so" — Christians know that evil will dominate the world until the final day, knowing that God remains in charge, but with a divine, not human time-table. Precisely because Christ is the center of time Christians know that they will be liberated from the mean, mean-time between birth and death, between Christ's first and second advent. While people play God, "He who sits in heaven laughs; the Lord has them in derision" (Ps. 2:4). The final Christian petition at the end of the Bible is, "Come, Lord Jesus!" (Rev. 22:20).

Have you thought about...

1. Why is the scale a good symbol for justice?
2. Compare and contrast the elements of law and justice.
3. How is it that a just law for some may be an unjust law for others?
4. Identify the instances of injustice in your community. How did you act in order to rectify the situation?
5. Relate an incident when you believe that you had been treated unjustly.

III
Baptism

Baptism is the initiation into the Christian community, the church, at any stage of life, be it right after birth (infant baptism) or later (adult baptism). If candidates are not adults, parents and/or sponsors stand in until the baptism is affirmed when candidates become adults (are educated to face life, drive a car, or join the army). Such "affirmation" (also called "confirmation") may, but need not become a special rite, preferably between sixteen and twenty-one years of age. Baptism is called a "sacrament:" a solemn rite of words and actions based on the mandate of Jesus, "Go and make disciples of all nations baptizing them" (Matt. 28:20). The key words are "I baptize you in the name of the Father, the Son and the Holy Spirit," accompanied by the use of water (immersion, pouring or at least sprinkling).

> "Why should I be baptized?", asked the woman who had gone church-shopping and found a congregation she liked (they had entertaining social activities, challenging programs and a good-looking female pastor). "I have my faith within me, pray to God and try to be a good person. Why this rite of ancient times?" The pastor replied, "Baptism is a visible, public sign of victory in the struggle against evil until Christ returns to establish a never-ending reign of love." "Are you telling me that I have to join a struggle when I get baptized?" "Yes," said the pastor, "and you will receive the power of God's Spirit to survive, supported by other active members of the congregation." "Well," the woman said. "I am just curious enough to see whether you are right." She was baptized.

The biblical tradition affirms a wholistic view of life, without any separation of internal and external features. The Greek and Roman view of life tended to be dualistic, based on the teachings of the Greek philosopher Aristotle (384-322 B.C.). Accordingly, there is an external, perishable body and an invisible, eternal soul which leaves the body after its death and returns to the eternal realm, from whence it came. It became popular to believe that the soul would leave the dying body through the mouth at one's last gasp. But the Bible means by "soul" the very being of a person as a whole ("the breath of life," Gen. 2:7). Thus any communication and encounter between people, or between human creatures and God, always involves the body as the most obvious, visible part of a person. So there is a "body-side" of God in human life, usually called the "spiritual" life, as a relationship with God in worship and ritual. The body-side of God in baptism is "washing" (or bathing), symbolized by water on the body, usually by immersion, or at least pouring water on the forehead. On the other hand, there is also God in Christ, embodied, incarnate, "enfleshed," as it were. A body takes up space and time, be it a body of literature or human bodies. Sacraments, like baptism, are embodiments of the Gospel, the good news of salvation in Christ.

The liturgy of baptism outlines the instruction for continuing education and spiritual formation: 1) *Daily struggle against evil* ("Do you renounce all the forces of evil?"); 2) *reliance on a shared faith* (joining the congregation in the confession of the Apostles' Creed); and 3) *using the gift of the Holy Spirit* ("You have been sealed by the Holy Spirit and marked with the cross of Christ forever").[21]

DAILY STRUGGLE AGAINST EVIL

Baptism creates visible membership in the church and commits to a never-ending struggle against the forces of evil (also called "exorcism").

> "My life is protected against evil," says the naïve, born-again Christian. "I dedicated myself to Jesus three years ago at an 'altar call' on a Friday evening at 9:00 p.m. in a big revival meeting. I love my country and pray that God

destroys its enemies. Many of my neighbors refuse to accept Christ as their Lord and will go to hell."

One is never born again just once, but again and again. Baptism commits to a daily struggle against evil, be it manifested in confusion, a drive to control others, or escape from daily duties. Baptism demands a serpentine, rational analysis of everyday life for the sake of identifying and renouncing any force of evil.

> [Baptism] signifies that the old creature in us with all sins and evil is to be drowned and die through daily contrition and repentance, and on the other hand that daily a new person is to come forth and rise up to live before God in righteousness and purity forever (Martin Luther).[22]

"Contrition" and "repentance" are not pietistic exercises of self-control through some kind of spiritual flagellation, be it by cloistered monks and nuns or by individual Christians who are plagued by anxiety over their imagined wrath of God against their sins. Rather, repentance is a true "change of mind" (*metanoia* in Greek) from fear to faith. As John the Baptist put it: "Repent, and believe in the good news" (*euangellion* in Greek, "gospel"). When minds get confused by evil, they can get lost unless they receive help from the outside. If advised to try harder with self-help ("pull yourself up by your own boot straps"), minds can become suicidal because they have no strength of their own any more to pull out of their anxiety. Returning the mind to baptism is the beginning of true penance. It is the way "'back to the future" because baptism receives its power from the future with God in Christ.

> Should we continue in sin in order that grace may abound? By no means! How can we who died to sin go on living in sin? Do you not know that all of us who have been baptized into Christ Jesus were baptized into his death? Therefore we have been buried with him by baptism into death, so that, just as Christ was raised from the dead by the glory of the Father, so we too may walk in newness of life (Rom. 6:1-4).

Reliance on a Shared Faith

Evil should never be fought on its own ground but from the high ground of the believing community where Christ promised to be present until he comes again to usher in his kingdom.

> "Let us do a Private (auricular) Confession," counsels the pastor who had had long discussion with a parishioner longing for a gracious God, but only feels the threat of divine wrath. After the parishioner confessed a long list of sins, the pastor pronounced the forgiveness of all the sins. "This is a closure," he told the parishioner. "Read your baptismal certificate as evidence that you are continuously born again through the Holy Spirit as the Spirit of Christ ('who proceeds from the Father and the Son', as the Nicene Creed asserts). Encounter the real presence of Christ in the Lord's Supper and ask friends to pray for you. This is the true penitential daily struggle against evil." The parishioner followed the advice and moved from self-pity to a therapeutic wrestling with existential problems, continually supported by reliable friends in the parish.

Few struggles can be conducted alone; perhaps only when no one is there to help. Soldiers, fire-fighters, baseball players or almost any significant effort in life needs teamwork. "Faith" is only effective when it is shared. It takes at least two to have faith; it is shared because one receives it and hands it on. Christ told his disciples that he would be with them when they have learned to rely on each other.

> If two or three agree on earth about anything you ask, it will be done for you by my Father in heaven. For where two or three are gathered in my name, I am there among them (Matt. 18:19-20).

That is why candidates for baptism are baptized in the worshipping assembly on Sunday (also often at the Easter Vigil before Easter

Sunday, an ancient tradition still cherished in Eastern Orthodoxy). Private baptisms should take place in emergencies, usually when candidates (often babies) are in deadly peril.

> "I am losing my faith in God," confesses one member of the church to another. "Do not be afraid," responds the other member. "I have sufficient faith for both of us. Just borrow from me until you feel strong again. No interest charged because Jesus Christ is my MasterCard."

Candidates for baptism are asked to adopt the faith of the church summarized in the Apostles' Creed. It is the assurance that the struggle against evil is a communal undertaking.

USING THE GIFT OF THE HOLY SPIRIT

The Holy Spirit is given in baptism like a seal that is imprinted on a formal document. It is given without conditions as the power of salvation from evil, whether the candidate wants it or not. No human effort can earn it, and not even baptism can guarantee it.

> "I was baptized to be saved from sin," one parent tells another. "Since your baby died without having been baptized, it is not saved and will go to hell." "Oh, no," responds the well-instructed Christian parent of the dead baby. "God still loves my baby though death surprised us before we could baptize. But God does not operate by human logic."

The Holy Spirit is given in baptism to assist in the daily struggle against evil, bonding with others in the struggle. Some baptized Christians do not use this powerful gift. Nevertheless, the power remains real and valid. But it is only beneficial when used in everyday life. Moreover, the gift also becomes a task: to care for others in need of love. Faith must become active in love, and the mind must discern the best ways to care for others in need. But such love is also marked by the cross, by some suffering, indeed pain. Christians who struggle through everyday life also feel pain and may meet opposition.

It is that very [Holy] Spirit bearing witness with our spirit that we are children of God, and if children, then heirs, heirs of God and joint heirs with Christ — if, in fact, we suffer with him so that we may also be glorified with him (Rom. 8: 16-17).

Christian suffering is not a way of penance to be rewarded by eternal joy. It is like the pain of athletes who endure it to become stronger, or the birth pangs of a mother, delivering new life. Being in training for Christian formation and for survival in everyday life involves therapeutic suffering — symbolized by the immersion into the water of baptism, threatening drowning, yet resulting in better spiritual breathing. If not grounded in baptism, spiritual formation is just a generic discipline, similar, if not identical, with self-centered exercises of minds and bodies.

During the first centuries of Christian history (and still in the Greek Orthodox Church today) the rite of initiation consisted of baptism, the Lord's Supper and confirmation: the baby or adult is baptized by immersion; then communed (with a mixture of bread and wine on a spoon for the baby) and finally confirmed by the use of consecrated oil applied to the forehead, the palms and the feet, symbolizing full acceptance in the church. Other rites, called "sacraments," were added to the two original ones, baptism and the Lord's Supper. Thus there were seven sacraments to protect believers from evil and confer upon them sacramental grace at decisive stages of life, from cradle to grave: baptism, shortly after birth; confirmation at age seven as the prerequisite of Holy Communion; Holy Communion, penance, with emphasis on private confession; marriage; ordination; and last rites before death. Only priests, with the minimum age of twenty-five, male, celibate and ordained by a bishop, were authorized to enact sacraments, except baptism which could also be enacted by non-ordained Christians.

The ancient (and Greek Orthodox) inclusion of the Lord's Supper into baptism and its affirmation or confirmation recommends itself to this handbook as a powerful third stage of spiritual formation in the 21st century (besides the diagnosis of evil and the work for justice). Such a change would also reduce a tradition of pious anxiety which tries to control the power of baptism and the Lord's Supper through numerous regulations enforced by an authoritarian hierarchy of officers, or through moral conditions based on spiritually dangerous notions of "worthiness."

Have you thought about...

1. Consider how your life may be different if you had never been baptized.
2. How would you describe the power of baptism to a child or a non-believer?
3. As a member of a congregation, how seriously do you take your own promises required in the service of baptism? How do you follow through with your promises?
4. Why do we need to reaffirm our baptism each day, as Luther instructs?
5. How do you use the gift of the Holy Spirit that was given to you in your baptism?

IV
THE CHURCH

The church is the gathering of those who are baptized, reaffirm their faith and commune. The celebration of the Lord's Supper in public worship, generally on Sunday when the resurrection of Jesus is remembered, is the most important feature of the church. Linked to the visible presence of Christ, members help and support each other in order to remain strong and faithful. The church is like a human body in which all members are to function for the good of the whole, with Christ being the head.

> For just as the body is one and has many members, and all the members of the body, though many, are one body, so it is with Christ. For in the one Spirit we were all baptized into one body — Jews and Greeks, slaves or free — and we are all made to drink of one Spirit (1 Cor. 12:12-13).

> [Christ] is the head of the body, the church (Col. 1:18).

But the church is visible, exposed to evil and is struggling for survival, just as all its members do. That is why the church is often called "militant" or "in conflict" (over against the "church triumphant" when earthly life has come to an end).

The ancient Nicene Creed defines the church as "one, holy, catholic and apostolic." This Handbook discusses the one church as 1) *holy*, 2) *catholic* and 3) *apostolic*.

HOLY

"Holy" means belonging to God; it does not mean to have any special moral superiority. The "communion of saints," as the ancient church described itself, are people who know whose they are. Like astronauts on a space walk, they are connected to the lifelines of the space ship. Their lifelines are word and sacrament which connect them to the captain of the ship, the resurrected Jesus, who directs and supervises their mission in a strange, dangerous environment. The Bible uses the analogy of a holy building, a temple.

> You are members of the household of God, built upon the foundation of the prophets and apostles, with Christ himself as the corner-stone. In him the whole structure is joined together and grows into a holy temple in the Lord, in whom you are also built together spiritually into a dwelling place for God (Eph. 2:19-22).

The church is holy because God dwells in it and supports it through the continual witness of the Bible as the means for communicating God's love, first for Israel through "prophets" (from the Greek *prophetes*, "messenger") and then for the whole world through "apostles" (from the Greek *apostolos*, "emissary"). The prophets and the apostles portray a God who creates, sustains and returns human creatures from their idolatry to their original place with God.[23] Grounded in this prophetic and apostolic witness, the ancient church proclaims that unconditional trust in Christ is the means by which one becomes right with God. Thus the core of the authority of the Bible is the assertion that "the righteous live by their faith" (Hab. 2:4. Rom. 1:17). The church is called to be a gathering of those who have heard this promise and stake their lives on it; this is the source of the church's holiness.

Neither the church as an institution, with all its necessary features for the sake of effective witness and service in the world, nor the Bible in all its complex parts, are in themselves holy. Should ancient customs recorded in the Bible become contemporary holy mandates, like polygamy? Should Jewish holiness codes become universal laws, like the prohibition of certain foods such as pork (Lev. 11:7)? The apostle Paul and other authors of pastoral epistles would be surprised, indeed angry, if they knew that many Christians make their letters into channels of unchanging divine revelations about Christian life in the past two millennia. Is the husband "the head of his wife?" (1 Cor. 11:3). Should women never be permitted to teach? (1 Tim. 2:12). "Anyone unwilling to work should not eat" (2 Thess. 3:10). If every word of the Bible were authoritative the manger in which Jesus was born would be a divinely mandated place of birth! When Paul wrote to Timothy, "All scripture is inspired by God," he meant the Old Testament as the Bible for Israel. He never viewed himself as a divinely inspired author who is enthroned above others.

> What then is Apollos? What is Paul? I planted, Apollos watered, but God gave the growth. So neither the one who plants nor the one who waters is anything, but only God who gives the growth (1 Cor. 3:5-7).

The Bible is the freezer, as it were, which preserves the original Christian witness of the Word of God regarding the destiny of the people of God, the Church, throughout the world. The Word of God is "audible" — proclaimed and heard; it is also "visible" (as St. Augustine calls it) — seen and experienced as sacrament.[24] In a world marked by evil, sin and death, the Word of God is both "law" and "gospel": the law, encountered in basic mandates like the Ten Commandments, prevents chaos and discloses the limits of sinful human power; the "gospel" is the good news about Jesus as the only mediator of salvation. Law and gospel are like a red line running through the Bible, the line of the prophets of the Old Testament and line of the apostles of the New Testament. Both prophets and apostles portray a God who creates, sustains and returns human creatures from their idolatry to their original place with God, not to the first garden but to a new "city of God" (Hebr. 11:16). Any biblical law, even if it is totally fulfilled, does not save from sin, evils and death; only total trust in Christ does.

The post-biblical tradition shows how the Word of God was thawed and communicated in twenty centuries. It is a history of incredible complexity ranging from a contradictory variety of ecclesiastical teachings to the persecution, indeed slaughter, of many innocents in the world. The main reason for such a scandalous history of Christian morality is the lack of serpentine wisdom which creates the necessary discipline for the church to continue its trek through an evil world. Such serpentine wisdom must always distinguish law and gospel. Complete trust in God's guidance of the church through unconditional faith in Christ must be combined with the cold-blooded work of the mind to diagnose and treat the diseases of evil with protective laws. These laws oppose the power of evil, centered in idolatry, the continual temptation "to be like God" (Gen. 3:5), violating the divine mandate to "have no other gods" (Ex. 20:3). *There are no other unchanging eternally guaranteed mandates, laws, moral rules or ethical principals during the life in this world.* There are, to be sure, enduring mandates, above all the discipline of spiritual formation, to generate the best possible attitude for Christian witness and service in the world where "we see in a mirror dimly" (1 Cor. 13:12). But the ancient prophetic advice is serpentine wisdom for every generation:

> He [God] has told you, O mortal, what is good; and what does the Lord require of you but to do justice, and to love kindness, and to walk humbly with your God? (Micah 6:8).

No specific forms of justice, of kindness and of humility create "eternal" goodness" in this world. The ever-present temptation to be "like God" (Gen. 3:5) confuses good and evil. What one society labels as "good" can easily become "evil" and vice-versa. That is why the church and its life on earth must be continually reformed; otherwise the church becomes God's "frozen people" whose holiness will be transformed into a hypocritical piety.

Among devastating manifestations of such a piety is anti-Semitism which has split the biblical people of God into Jews, who allegedly have forfeited the blessings of God by killing Jesus, and Christians, who are the "new Israel", now the only people of God. But this conclusion is the result of a scapegoat ideology which targets the people of Israel as the source of many calamities in the world, revealing God's wrath. So they supposedly must be converted or segregated, indeed eradicated, a conclusion which created a Christian "mission to the Jews" and a racist holocaust.

But the people of God continue to be both Israel and the church; it remains a divine mystery why Israel has not yet affirmed Christ as the promised Messiah.

> I want you to understand this mystery: a hardening of heart has come upon part of Israel, until the full number of the Gentiles has come in. And so all Israel will be saved.... As regards the gospel they are enemies of God for your sake, but as regards election they are beloved, for the sake of their ancestors; for the gifts and the calling of God are irrevocable.... O the depth of the riches and wisdom and knowledge of God! How unsearchable are his judgments and how inscrutable his ways! (Rom. 11:25-26, 28-29, 33).

CATHOLIC

"Catholic" means "common" and "universal." Thus the church must be united around the world, not in uniformity but in reconciled diversity. But visible Christian unity is an ideal without much reality. Christian communities always tend to drift apart because of differences which become norms and exclude others. But Christians must be united in their link to God through Christ who prayed for unity before he left the earth.

> Holy Father, protect them in your name that you have given me, so that they may be one, as we are one (John 17:11).

Already the apostle Paul encountered quarrels and divisions in his congregations. Some advocated a "Pauline" church, others a "Petrine" one (1 Cor. 3:21). He called for unity in essentials.

> There is one body and one Spirit, just as you were called to the one hope of your calling, one Lord, one faith, one baptism, one God and Father of all, who is above all and through all. But each of us was given grace according to the measure of Christ's gift (Eph. 4:4-7).

It is the task of spiritual formation to seek and achieve unity in the Word of God, offered through basic rules and rites, word and sacraments. Such matters as budget, polity, theology and other arrangements may vary from church to church. Christians around the world must be united in essentials and enjoy non-essentials according to what seems best for a faithful witness at specific times and in specific places.

> The unity of the Church is the commandment of the Lord of the Church, who will demand from the leaders of the churches an accounting as to whether or not they have really done everything possible in this matter (Heinrich Fries and Karl Rahner, 1983).[25]

APOSTOLIC

"Apostolic" means "sent." The church exists for its mission to show the world a glimpse of the future that is to come when evil will be no more. Thus the church is a living advertisement of such "good news." (from the Greek *euangellion*, "gospel"). Every baptized member is a minister of the gospel, based on baptism; but some must be elected to lead, like in every earthly organization; otherwise there is chaos.

> All things should be done decently and in order (1 Cor. 14:40).

> The gifts he [Christ] gave were that some would be apostles, some prophets, some evangelists, some pastors and teachers, to equip the saints for the work of ministry (Eph. 4:11-12).

> You are a chosen race, a royal priesthood, a holy nation, God's own people, in order that you may proclaim the mighty acts of him who called you out of darkness into his marvelous light (1 Peter 2:9).

The mission of the church determines its structure, be it headed by "bishops" (from the Greek *episcopos*, "overseer") or by other chosen leaders. Function determines structure. Whatever is best for being sent is best for the church. Here is a place for much critique and reform. Some churches exist without a sense of sin and suffering; they are voluntary associations of people in comfortable pews, listening to sermons uncritical of a selfish style of life and unconcerned about the absence of Christ on non-eucharistic altars. H. Richard Niebuhr (1894-1962) spoke satirically about the sad lack of mission and conviction in American denominations which show no repentance for their faults: "A God without wrath brought people without sin into a kingdom without judgment through the ministrations of a Christ without a cross."[26] The flashy revivalist Billy Sunday (1862-1935) offered his own, unique description of Christians in need of conversion: "Hog-jowled, weasel-eyed, sponge-columned, mushy-fisted, jelly-spined, pussy-footing, four-flushing, Charlotte-russe Christians."[27]

The church has a sad record of being called, united and sent to represent its Lord Jesus Christ. A lack of serpentine wisdom, a gospel-romanticism and idealistic attempts to create the kingdom of God on earth have made the church often a victim of evil. That is why the church must always be reformed, reshaped and renewed for its mission to embody the severe struggle between the forces of evil and the power of the Holy Spirit.

> Present your bodies as a living sacrifice, holy and acceptable to God, which is your reasonable worship. Do not be conformed to this world, but be transformed by the renewing of your minds, so that you may discern what is the will of God — what is good and acceptable and perfect (Rom. 12:1-23).

Have you thought about...

1. What are the essential elements of the church?
2. Considering the variety of churches, what are the advantages and disadvantages of diversity?
3. What characteristics of the church attract you? What characteristics repel you?
4. What is the role of the Bible in the church?
5. Elaborate on whether or not the church makes a difference in today's world?

V
THE LORD'S SUPPER

The Lord's Supper is also known through other designations: as "Communion," (from the Latin *communio*, "a sharing"); as "Eucharist" (from the Greek *eucharistia*, "Thanksgiving," a designation of the liturgical center in the celebration leading to the "Words of Institution" beginning with "This is my body", also known as "The Great Thanksgiving"); and as "Mass" (probably from the Latin dismissal formula in the Roman liturgy, *ita missa est*, telling visitors to leave before the celebration of the Lord's Supper by committed, baptized members).

This sacrament is based on the last meal of Jesus with his disciples which he commanded them to re-enact in their common worship until he comes again.

> The Lord Jesus in the night in which he was betrayed took a loaf of bread and when he had given thanks, he broke it and said, "This is my body that is broken for you. Do this in remembrance of me." In the same way he took the cup also, after supper, saying, "This cup is the new covenant in my blood. Do this, as often as you drink it, in remembrance of me. For as often as you eat this bread and drink the cup, you proclaim the Lord's death until he comes" (1 Cor. 11:23-26).

The Lord's Supper is the most significant, yet also most controversial, event in Christian history. Its interpretations have made the blood of many theologians run cold, and its celebrations have symbolized division rather than unity. Controversies range from elaborate attempts to explain Christ's "real presence," or even "real absence," to questions of who is authorized to preside at the eucharistic celebration, or who should be excluded from participation. But the Lord's Supper is the very center of spiritual formation because it establishes the closest relationship between Christ and his followers. In the eucharistic meal he shares himself through bread and wine, thus becoming an intimate part of Christian life. That is why the church was soon called "the body of Christ."

Three aspects are essential for spiritual formation: 1) *the presence of* Christ, 2) *interim food* and 3) *a foretaste of the feast to come.* These are indispensable sources for the core of Christian life in an evil world.

THE PRESENCE OF CHRIST

In the eucharistic "liturgy" (from the Greek *leitourgia,* "public service," also "the work of the people") Christ is present in the words and in the meal of bread and wine (distributed in small amounts). It makes no difference whether participants believe that this is so. Skeptics or non-believers also encounter Christ's true presence. Just like the sacrament of baptism conveys the Holy Spirit, so does "the Sacrament of the Altar" make Christ truly present without any precondition, not even faith. Thus the sacrament is valid, no matter whether the celebrant or communicants believe it. But Christ does not invade, as it were, unbelievers; they must invite him into their lives at the eucharistic meal in order to receive its benefits.

> "Christ cannot be in two places at the same time," declares the rationalist. "How can we say in the same church service in our confession of the Nicene Creed that he is 'seated at the right hand of the Father' and then find him also in the bread and in the cup? Why not just remember his last meal on specific holidays and celebrate the Eucharist just on a few Sundays?" "Why worry about such scientific contradictions?" responds a pious mind. "Christ is only spiritually present through the Holy Spirit by faith, and we encounter him that way while we eat the bread and sip the wine." "But Christ is truly present wherever and however he wishes to be present," asserts

a well-catechized listening by-stander, "because he is the Son of God, 'true God from true God', as we also confess in the Creed."

The sacrament of baptism hooks Christians up, so to speak, with the resurrected Christ and puts them on the road to freedom from sin, evil and death. The Lord's Supper supplies regular contact and nourishment at least every Sunday when the church remembers Christ's resurrection. That is why baptized Christians of all ages can participate in the Lord's Supper.

> Age limits were imposed in the medieval Roman Catholic Church by the Fourth Lateran Council of 1215 because of its focus on "holy things" — the consecrated bread and wine. Only priests could handle the "sacramental elements." One has to be seven years old, go to confession and be "confirmed" before one can receive the holy elements. Remaining consecrated bread had to be "reserved" in a special container ("tabernacle"); and the remaining wine had to be consumed by the priest who had an "indelible quality" (*character indelebilis* in Latin). But since the Lord's Supper is also a liturgical event it also uses "holy time," not just "holy things." *Both* constitute the Eucharist. That is why it is often extended to commune the sick who are not in the church and are communed by deacons or other appointed assistants. When the Eucharist ends all its "elements" become again what they were before, ordinary time, bread and wine.

There is no ecumenical agreement about the proper nature and function of ordination. According to ancient custom, ordained members of the church preside at the public Sunday worship, consisting of a service of word and sacrament, ranging from preaching to speaking in tongues (1 Cor. 14:26-40). The power of ordination was not exclusively linked to the consecration and distribution of bread and wine in public and private worship. Ordained pastors were elected or appointed to be leaders of congregations or other communities. Everything, including worship, was to be "done decently and in good order" (1 Cor.14:40). Since baptism makes all members of the church spiritually equal, any baptized member may preside when an ordained member cannot be present. But whatever is liturgically arranged is guided by the mandate, "Let all things be done for building up" (1 Cor. 14:26).

Among the hosts of interpretations and controversies over the sacramental presence of Christ, one such quarrel has even produced a new phrase.

> The abuse of the Latin "Words of Institution" (also known as the "Canon of the Mass") has created the phrase "hocus-pocus" — *hoc est meum corpus*, "this is my body." Medieval priests spoke the words so fast that the uneducated, often illiterate, common people thought they heard *hocus-pocus*, a phrase also later used by magicians. Since the church taught that only priests could "transubstantiate" the resurrected Jesus into consecrated bread and wine just by using the words, they appeared to have become ecclesiastical magicians.[28]

But all attempts to explain Christ's presence run aground in the face of Christ's promise that he would be truly present with his disciples in the bread and wine, the peculiar essential nourishment offered in the ancient Jewish feast of Passover, commemorating the exodus from Egypt (Exod.12). The gathering in the Lord's Supper also recalls the sacrifice of Jesus ("the lamb of God," John 1:29). The words in the celebration become a mandate ("Do this...," 1 Cor. 11:24) and should be obeyed, not doubted and debated.

Dietrich Bonhoeffer pleaded for unity in the Lord's Supper between the Lutheran and Reformed (Calvinist) churches in Germany:

> Christ is more important than our thoughts of him and his presence. Both are theologically questionable foundations for unity, and yet the church decided in faith for eucharistic, that is, inter-church communion. It decided

to recognize the union as the guiding hand of God, and it decided to subordinate its ideas or doctrine about Christ to the objectivity of the presence of Christ.[29]

Interim Food

The weekly (and sometimes daily) celebration of the Lord's Supper is the basic diet for spiritual formation. The words and actions of the celebration link believers to Christ as the liberator from evils that beset them throughout their life on earth. Survivors cherish the saving protection from danger and death, be it a rope in the climbing of mountains or the life-preserver in dangerous waters. Linked to Christ as their mediator of salvation they themselves offer their lives for service in the world, fed with "heavenly food."

> The Church earnestly desires that Christ's faithful, when present at this mystery of faith, should not be there as strangers or silent spectators. On the contrary, through a good understanding of the rites and prayers they should take part in the sacred action, conscious of what they are doing, with devotion and full collaboration. They should be instructed in God's word, and be nourished at the table of the Lord's Body. They should give thanks to God. Offering the immaculate victim, not only through the hands of the priest but also together with him, they should learn to offer themselves. Through Christ, the Mediator, they should be drawn day by day into ever more perfect union with God and each other, so that finally God may be God in all" (Second Vatican Council, 1963).[30]

Besides the Sunday celebrations of the Lord's Supper, there are also specific occasions to provide it as food for spiritual formation and discipline during the interim pilgrimage on earth: when a dangerous illness strikes; at the hour of death; at baptism, at a wedding or on other significant occasions. The Lord's Supper is the most significant event because Christ is present, using space and time in the eucharistic meal of bread and wine. He is not present like an invisible ghost, or as a memorial, but as the Lord of his church. Bread and wine are real food recalling the survival of the people of God in the desert of Egypt. Together with baptism, the Lord's Supper discloses the divine love which conquers evil in Jesus and provides the means for survival: water, bread and wine; bread and water for survival in the desert of life, and wine for joyful celebration and thanksgiving. That is why the Lord's Supper is often followed by an "Agape Meal" (from the Greek *agape*, "non-erotic love") or "Love Feast." It links Christians with each other as well as with others who are poor, hungry and lonely.

A Foretaste of the Feast to Come

The gathered Christians, the church, are on the way to a future without evil, sin and death. The Lord's Supper is a reminder of what happened when Jesus did his work of salvation; and it is a sign-post of the future reunion with him. The main parts of the Jewish Passover meal (in memory of the exodus from Egypt), bread, wine and prayer, become the sources for the spiritual formation needed to stay on track in the march to the end-time. In this sense, the celebration of the Eucharist becomes, as the "Offertory" in the eucharistic liturgy declares, "a foretaste of the feast to come."

> Let the vineyards be fruitful, Lord, and fill to the brim our cup of blessing. Gather a harvest from the seeds that were sown, that we may be fed with the bread of life. Gather the hopes and dreams of all; unite them with the prayers we offer. Grace our table with your presence, and give us a foretaste of the feast to come.[31]

The Lord's Supper is the most concrete way in which Christ guides and sustains his followers during the time between his first and second advent.

> Jesus said to them, "I have eagerly desired to eat this Passover with you before I suffer; for I tell you, I will not eat it again until it is fulfilled in the kingdom of God" (Luke 22:14, 18).

As interim food, it is also the most tangible way to experience God's incarnation in Christ as the mediator of salvation in flesh and blood, as well as in bread and wine. Its celebration should reflect the stages of spiritual formation, sometimes coordinated with the basic features of the Christian liturgical calendar: a meditative Advent symbolizing the coming of Christ as the child of Mary and as the Lord of the end-time; a joyous Christmas, celebrating the birth of Jesus; a reflective Lent and Easter, anticipating suffering and liberation from death; and a grateful Pentecost, the birthday of the church through the gifts of the Holy Spirit to the pilgrim people of God marching into a future with a never-ending union with God through Christ. Thus the Lord's Supper mirrors penitential change, anticipation, joy, hope and other components of spiritual formation in all ways of everyday life.

Have You Thought About...

1. What do you remember about your first communion?
2. In what ways have your views of the Lord's Supper changed?
3. What benefits do you receive by participating in the Lord's Supper?
4. How would you rate the importance of Holy Communion in relation to the other aspects of worship?
5. Describe the Eucharistic features that raise questions for you.

VI
Prayer

Prayer is both the simplest and most direct communication with God. Praying may be endless ("Pray without ceasing," 1 Thess. 5:17) or, in an emergency believers sometimes end up with a "spiritual ejaculation," as it were, exclaiming or muttering a kind of "911" signal for help such as "Jesus, help me!" Very disciplined believers use prayers of intercession which they prepare with great care, or even know by heart. There is a solid ecumenical tradition (called "evangelical-catholic"), consisting of believers, usually clergy, who pray several times a day. They use set prayers connected with the reading of a daily lectionary. To them it is a discipline that affords them time to listen to God speaking in Scripture and in the "saints" of the Church. This is a meditative way to develop spiritual formation.[32]

Since God was incarnate in Jesus, who consoled, healed and even resurrected some who had died, prayers are addressed to him as the best source for help since he had conquered sin, evil and death. He promised to be with his disciples on their trek through earthly life "to the end of the age" (Matt. 28:20).

> For in him [Jesus] every one of God's promises is a 'Yes.' For this reason it is through him that we say 'Amen,' to the glory of God (2 Cor. 1:20).

> Be alert at all times, praying that you may have the strength to escape all these things that will take place, and to stand before the Son of Man" (Luke 21:36).

Prayer is also the safety valve, as it were, for spiritual formation when frustration, impatience or any other emotional pressures need to be vented. Such prayers constitute a portion of the biblical

Psalms, the most illustrative collection of prayers ranging from humble bidding requests to "bitching" complaints.

> Hear the voice of my supplication, as I cry to you for help, as I lift up my hands toward your most holy sanctuary. Do not drag me away with the wicked, with those who are workers of evil (Ps. 28:2-3).

> Why have you forgotten me? Why must I walk about mournfully because the enemy oppresses me? As with a deadly wound my enemies taunt me, while they say to me continually, "Where is your God?" (Ps. 42:9-10).

Prayer is the most liberal feature of spiritual formation. When everything else seems to fail in the struggle for survival in a confusing world, praying is the first and last resort. Integrated in a program of spiritual formation, prayer is 1) *a lifeline to God*, 2) *guidance for survival*, and 3) *thanksgiving and praise*.

A Life-Line to God

Whereas baptism and the Lord's Supper are God's supply-lines to the Christian life in an evil world, prayer is the life-line from the Christian to God. Anything can be asked for, yet nothing is guaranteed. Divine clues, indeed answers to prayers, are often disclosed through other people. But essentially, the ways of God must be accepted as unsearchable.

> "For my thoughts are not your thoughts, nor are your ways my ways," says the Lord (Is. 55:8).

> How unsearchable are his judgments and how inscrutable his ways! For who has known the mind of the Lord? Or who has been his counselor? Or who has given a gift to him, to receive a gift in return? (Rom. 11:33-35).

Nevertheless, praying belongs to Christian life, and God will decide what should be granted through prayer. Some things may be granted, even though prayer did not ask for them. That is why the model prayer of Jesus, *The Lord's Prayer* (Matt.6: 9-13), begins with the praise of God ("hallowed be your name"), asks for the advent of the end-time ("your kingdom come") and accepts God's way ("your will be done").

> "I pray only when I am in trouble," says a pious but selfish parishioner. "For God helps only those who can no longer help themselves." "But then you only believe in the God of gaps," retorts the friend who has a regular prayer life. "Whenever you experience more than you can handle, you call on God to fill the gap between your weakness and divine strength. Yet God is in all the gaps."

Prayer is an essential part of spiritual formation. It involves the mind in order to assess what to pray for, and how to move from petition to action. That is why there are prayers that ask for clear thinking in times of confusion, addiction or doubt.

> An example is the prayer attributed to the American theologian Reinhold Niebuhr (1892-1971) used in meetings of Alcoholics Anonymous: "God grant me the Serenity to accept the things I cannot change; the Courage to change the things I can; and the Wisdom to know the difference."[33]

Guidance for Survival

The model petitions for survival on the pilgrimage from earthly life to the kingdom of God are offered in *The Lord's Prayer*: 1) For food from the earth to remain physically strong and healthy ("give us this day our daily bread"); 2) for mutual reconciliation so that the journey is not endangered by un-forgiven debts ("forgive us our debts as we have forgiven our debtors"); and 3) for rescue from paralyzing suffering through the trials of evil ("do not bring us to the time of trial, but rescue us from evil").

There also should be prayers of intercession for those who need help, be it in sickness or in any other tribulation. It is also important to pray for one another as members of the same community to keep it strong in its tasks. Above all, prayers should be honest without the selfish pride of listening to one's prayer skills or impress others with them.

> Pray in the Spirit at all times in every prayer and supplication. To that end keep alert and always persevere in supplication for all the saints (Eph. 67:18).

> Pray for one another, so that you may be healed (James 56:16).

> When you are praying, do not heap up empty phrases as the Gentiles do; for they think they will be heard because of their many words. Do not be like them, for your Father knows what you need before you ask him (Matt. 6:7-8).

THANKSGIVING AND PRAISE

Prayer asks for God's favors, indeed for God's saving interferences at times of danger, and gives thanks for what God has provided for the welfare of this world: government and family for law and order; changes and reforms for maintaining a good life; the gifts of nature, beauty or what ever other divine gifts help Christians to be of good cheer in their struggle for survival.

> I urge that supplications, prayers, intercessions and thanksgiving be made for everyone, for kings and all who are in high positions, so that we may lead a quiet and peaceable life in all godliness and dignity (1 Tim. 2:1-2).

> Joyfully giving thanks to the Father [who] has rescued us from the power of darkness and transferred us into the kingdom of his beloved Son, in whom we have redemption, the forgiveness of sins (Col. 1:12-14).

Praying is an integral part of worship when the public Christian assembly acknowledges the majesty of God, gives thanks for the presence of Christ in the liturgy and offers joyful praise to the love of God. Thanksgiving and praise should also be part of individual, personal prayers, be it for the birth of a child or the long, faithful life of a dying friend. Prayer exposes the depths and heights of spiritual formation.

Have you thought about...

1. Who taught you to pray?
2. What was your most significant prayer experience?
3. What are the advantages and/or disadvantages of a) praying alone? b) praying with others?
4. Evaluate your own prayer life.
5. What kind of prayer is most meaningful for you?

VII
Music

Music is an indispensable feature of human communication. The sound of music discloses surprising dimensions of human nature, ranging from depressing anxiety to liberating joy.

> Next to the Word of God music deserves the highest praise. She is a mistress and governess of those human emotions which as masters govern people or more often overwhelm them. No greater commendation than this can be found. For whether you wish to comfort the sad, to terrify the happy, to encourage the despairing, to humble the proud, to calm the passionate, or to appease those full of hate — and who could number all these masters of the human heart, namely the emotions, inclinations and affections that impel people to evil and good? — what more effective means than music could you find? The Holy Spirit himself honors her as an instrument for his proper work when in his holy Scriptures he asserts that through her his gifts were instilled in the prophets [2 Kings 3:15] On the other hand, she serves to cast out Satan, the instigator of all sins [Samuel 15:23] (Martin Luther).[34]

The struggle for Christian survival in an evil world needs to be cheered on by a harmony between the human spirit and the Holy Spirit as they move from earth and time to the "promised land." While the first six features of spiritual formation in this *Handbook* stress critical thinking, ranging from simple communication to complex doctrinal formulations, the final feature (music) provides an appropriate closure for the dialectic of serpenthood and dovehood.

There should be a time when sharp thinking breaks into song and serpentine wisdom becomes linked with dovehood-like doxology.

Three aspects make music an integral part of spiritual formation: 1) *Harmony and rhythm for the pilgrim church,* 2) *giving vent to emotions,* and 3) *an integral part of public worship.*

Harmony and Rhythm for the Pilgrim Church

Songs, musical instruments and rhythm, often expressed in dancing, have been visible marks of the biblical people of God since their earliest history. The transportation of the holy "ark of the covenant" to Jerusalem was accompanied by music and dance.

> David and all the house of Israel were dancing before the Lord with all their might, with songs and lyres and harps and tambourines and castanets and cymbals (2 Sam. 6:5).

The first generation of Christians were told to express their gratitude for God's unconditional love in Christ with music.

> Be filled with the Spirit, as you sing psalms and hymns and spiritual songs among yourselves, singing and making melody to the Lord in your hearts, giving thanks to God the Father at all times and for everything in the name of our Lord Jesus Christ" (Eph. 5:18-20).

As the church moves to the end-time it needs to be strengthened by music, created in the midst of spiritual struggle, or composed as a sound of praise. Every new movement of change, Christian or non-Christian, is cheered on by music. Marching is always made easier through music. Many Christian hymns attest to that. They provide the rhythm for the march of the church through the ages. Some hymns sound like marching songs of a purpose-driven movement.

Lift high the cross, the love of Christ proclaim,
till all the world adore his sacred name (Refrain).
Come, Christians follow where our captain trod,
our king victorious, Christ the Son of God.

All new-born soldiers of the Crucified
bear on their bows the seal of him who died.
So shall our song of triumph be:
Praise to the Crucified for victory!"[35]

GIVING VENT TO EMOTIONS

Human nature generates a great variety of emotions which, at times, seem uncontrollable or contrived. Unless clearly identified with a cause or purpose, emotions puzzle, indeed bewilder people inside and outside the church. Noisy revival meetings as well as continual silence have become part of Christian behavior. Whether I am a football fan or participate in a Christian revival meeting, the emotions are the same. Only when they are embodied in discernable words or expression (praising or scolding a particular football team, or screaming, "Praise the Lord!") does the difference become known. A visitor to a Quaker worship event was puzzled by the absence of a customary liturgical order; he did not know that the strict discipline of "The Society of Friends" (so named by their founder George Fox [1624-1691]) required silent worship as part of a life dedicated to the love of neighbor; sometimes the silence was broken by uncontrollable physical shaking or quaking attributed to the power of the Holy Spirit. But this meeting remained silent. "When does the service begin," the visiting stranger asked a Quaker sitting next to him. "When this is over, my friend," was the surprising response.

Christian revivalists view a number of biblical "spiritual gifts," called "charisms" (from the Greek *charisma*, "gift of grace") as sources of emotional "mountain top experiences," or spiritual "highs." The favorite gift is "speaking in tongues," also known as "glossolalia" (from the Greek *lalein*, "childish chattering"). The presence of such gifts is celebrated with a massive vent of emotions, manifested in agitating preaching, noisy assemblies and even in trance. But a song, or other disciplined musical expressions are more appropriate ways of attesting to the power of the Holy Spirit. Spiritual gifts must build up, not divide, the church.

> Now there are a variety of gifts, but the same Spirit.... To each is given the manifestation of the Spirit for common good... [healing, prophecy, speaking in tongues, etc.] (1 Cor. 12:4, 7-10).
>
> There are doubtless many different kinds of sounds in the world, and nothing is without sound. If then I do not know the meaning of a sound, I will be a foreigner to the speaker and the speaker a foreigner to me. So with yourselves; since you are eager for spiritual gifts, strive to excel in them for building up the church (1 Cor. 14:10-12).

Music provides a common discipline for venting the great variety of faithful emotions. Voices and musical instruments can convey laughter and sadness, anxiety and joy, despair and hope. They communicate the Word of God better than do unrestrained revival meetings, or charismatic cacophonies of individuals and groups. An African American Spiritual is a good example of giving vent to deep spiritual emotions with a disciplined focus on Christ as the living Word of God.

> There is a balm in Gilead to make the wounded whole;
> there is a balm in Gilead to heal the sin-sick soul" (Refrain).
> Sometimes I feel discouraged and think my work's in vain,
> but then the Holy Spirit revives my soul again.
> If you cannot preach like Peter, if you cannot pray like Paul,
> you can tell the love of Jesus and say, "He died for all."
> Don't ever feel discouraged, for Jesus is your friend;
> and if you lack for knowledge he'll ne'er refuse to lend.[36]

Hymns, solos of trumpets, violins, drums and bag-pipes can express the whole range of human emotions grounded in faith; and orchestras, organs, choirs and soloists can dominate the air with their expressions of Christian convictions grounded in the Word of God. This stance is exemplified in a well-known hymn of the Danish Lutheran churchman Nicolai Frederik Severin Grundtvig (1783-1872).

> God's Word is our great heritage,
> and shall be ours forever.
> To spread its light from age to age
> shall be our chief endeavor.
> Through life it guides our way;
> in death it is our stay.
> Lord, grant while time shall last,
> Your Church may hold it fast
> Throughout all generations.[37]

But doxology is often born in conflict. At almost every age voices within and outside the church have vented their frustration, impatience and even anger about the lack of spiritual care for hearts and minds in the twilight of faith and despair. Today, they compose music and lyrics in ways never heard before. But their sounds and words are spiritually powerful, exemplified by Shawn Jones, front-man of the seminal hardcore band "Zao," who cries out, "We've been made by the Maker, bought by the Buyer, broken by the Breaker… I am His." Such sentiment echoes the young Martin Luther who felt deceived by the church and was reduced to nothing but surrender to God's grace. The band "Zao" released widely influential albums such as *The Funeral of God* and *Where Blood and Fire Bring Rest*. The sound is irritating and often cacophonous, venting emotions of anger and despair. Atheists and agnostics claim to have become Christians after listening to rock bands like "Underoath" and "Mineral." The latter's music and lyrics are simple, honest and touching.

> I walked along beside the purple mountains
>   beneath the orange sky

Imagined what it all might look like with these planks
    out of my eyes.
I wondered if the big white horse was coming down tonight.
I wanted to taste that victory but my mouth was dry.
There is only tonight and the light that bleeds
    from your heart
Makes me want to try and start again.

And I know I don't deserve this, the capacity to feel,
To laugh and cry and to praise.
For that I live and breathe and wake each day
Is nothing less than your grace in awkward
    and glorious movement.

I wouldn't mind if you took me in my sleep tonight.
I wouldn't even put up a fight.
I wouldn't care if you took it all away today.
I'm sure I wouldn't even miss the pain.

But I know I've got to live my life
And roll around on the ground and feel the strife
And realize along the way that I'm nothing more
Than a grain of salt in the salt of the earth
And everything is grace.[38]

An Integral Part of Worship

Music has always been part of corporate Christian worship in one form or another. A particular way of chanting became the model of communication in the celebration of the Lord's Supper, eventually joined by congregational singing, choirs and musical performances. Pope Gregory I (590-604) was credited, but without solid evidence, with the origin of the "Gregorian Chant," a mixture of singing and speaking in order to limit any domination of emotion either by words or music. The chants were to express the Word of God, mostly biblical, to enhance the Scripture lessons and preaching. Organ music was used from the very beginning of Christian worship, but refined in the 17th and 18th centuries. Martin Luther (1483-1546) provided hymns for the people, making the Word of God into a song to be heard in the world. Johann Sebastian Bach (1685-1750) towers in the Christian tradition of joyful choral and organ music in his composition of the *Easter Oratorio*, the *Magnificat* and the *Toccata in F Minor*. Among the most performed works is the *Messiah*, Part III by George Frederick Handel (1685-1759). Modern Christian music offers Jazz Masses, country and a variety of other sounds.

Liturgy is enhanced by music and creates community by carefully chosen words and sounds. Hymns for the festivals of the church year, from Advent to Pentecost, constitute a special body of music. The ecumenical monastic community in Taize (since 1944 in Burgundy, France) composed a simple, catching hymn sung around the world during the eucharistic meal.

> Eat this bread, drink this cup,
> come to me and never be hungry.
> Eat this bread, drink this cup,
> trust in me and you will not thirst."[39]

Music, at its best, lifts the human spirit to great spiritual heights — from rational serpenthood to artistic dovehood as the best means for a wholesome everyday life.

Have you thought about...

1. What does music do for you?
2. How does music enhance or diminish the worship service for you?
3. Describe your comfort level when considering various types of music.
4. What defines "Christian music"?
5. What is your favorite piece of church music?

Conclusion

Christians must always focus on the biblical image of the church as a pilgrim people during the interim between the first and second advent of Christ. Consequently, the Christian life is marked by a peculiar freedom and doxological joy. It is the joyful freedom of believers who "have tasted the goodness of the Word of God and the powers of the age to come" (Hebr. 6:5). Their reality check of *evil* and *justice* shows them the abyss that separates them from God. But they also receive the Holy Spirit in *baptism* as the initiation into the *church* where Christ is present in the *Lord's Supper*. They know how powerful *prayer* can be when they read in the Bible how the first disciples of Jesus proclaimed the good news about the future with Christ, healed the sick and even resurrected the dead (Acts 9:36-41). That is why Christians oftentimes say that *music* transports them into another realm.

Death is a reminder of the need for quality time; and the resurrection of Jesus opens the door to a life without end. Human creatures exist between birth and death as the brief interim imbedded in a longer one marked by Christ's first and second coming. Such interim existence is often ignored, even by serious Christians who have yielded to life in the fast track of history. To be sure, some have become speed-sick and have left the track to catch their spiritual breath. Others just try to survive by going with the flow of life as they encounter it. The church, too, has often abandoned its original interim style of life and has succumbed to the siren song of institutional triumphalism marked by the strife for comfortable "mega churches" or cozy otherworldly conventicles. There is a hard drive for mission by numbers—a cowboy/girl view of ministry with the slogan, "Find them, corral them, count them and brand them as the property of Christ."

This *Handbook* calls for a renewal of the classical Christian interim attitude: life between the ascension of Jesus and his return, "the day of the Lord [which] will come like a thief in the night'" (1 Thess. 5:2). Only the quintessential features for contemporary spiritual formation are offered in this *Handbook*. It starts from scratch, as it were, positioning the mind for the best possible start in the brief run of life (as did the short-distance runners in the ancient Olympic games by using one foot to scratch for solid ground to start). When a group of such starters is assembled the spiritual formation begins. *But it must be done with a well-developed and constantly refined sense of serpenthood and dovehood:* a diagnosis of obstacles, a spiritual conditioning, and an enduring stamina of faith with a sense of joy in everyday life.

  This *Handbook* is ecumenical with a common sense, sharpened by life in the 21st century, for the ancient, apostolic call to become "servants of Christ and stewards of God's mysteries" (1 Cor. 4:1).

References

1. Buckminster Fuller, *Operating Manual for Spaceship Earth*, 1963.
2. Martin Luther, *The Small Catechism* in Robert Kolb and Timothy J. Wengert, eds., *The Book of Concord. The Confessions of the Evangelical Lutheran Church* (Minneapolis: Fortress Press), pp. 347-64.
3. Erasmus of Rotterdam calls it "dagger" in *Handbook (Enchiridion) of the Militant Christian* (1503). Roland H. Bainton, *Erasmus of Christendom* (New York: Charles Scribner's Sons, 1969), p. 66.
4. *Book of Concord*, p. 347.
5. "Enchiridia" as hymnals. *Luther's Works*. American Edition, 55 vols, Jaroslav Pelikan and Helmut Lehmann, eds. (Philadelphia: Fortress, St. Louis: Concordia, 1955-1986), 53, p. 193.
6. Robert W. Jenson, *A Large Catechism* (Delhi, NY: American Lutheran Publicity Bureau, 1991).
7. *Catechism of the Roman Catholic Church* (New York: Doubleday, 2003).
8. Luther, *The Small Catechism* in *The Book of Concord*, 347:2-348:3
9. Dietrich Bonhoeffer, *Ethics* (New York: Macmillan, 1955), pp. 21, 354.
10. Lutheranism is shown to be an ecumenical reform movement in Eric W. Gritsch and Robert W. Jenson, *Lutheranism: The Theological Movement and Its Confessional Writings* (Minneapolis: Fortress Press, 1976).
11. "Murphy's Law": The law or principle that if anything can go wrong, it will. Named after the American engineer Edward Murphy (1917-).
12. Luther's "Table Talk," No. 5010 in *Luther's Works*, 54, p. 377.
13. B. L. Rayner, *Life of Jefferson* (Boston, 1834), p. 356.
14. "Idle Mind" in H. G. Bohn, *Handbook of Proverbs* (1855).
15. "Fear" in Samuel Rosenman, ed., *The Public Papers of Franklin Delano Roosevelt*, Vol. II, *The Years of Crisis* (New York: Random House, 1938). Inaugural address, 1933, pp. 11-16.
16. M. L. King, Jr. (1929-1968), US African American civil rights leader and clergyman in *Letter From the Birmingham Jail*, April 16, 1963.
17. "I Wonder as I Wander" in *With One Voice: A Lutheran Resource for Worship* (Minneapolis: Augsburg Fortress, 1995), No. 642.
18. Joy to the World" in *Lutheran Book of Worship* (Minneapolis: Augsburg Publishing House, 1978), No. 39.
19. John Calvin, *Institutes of the Christian Religion* (1559) in Alister E. McGrath, ed., *The Christian Theology Reader*, 2nd ed. (Oxford: Blackwell, 2001).
20. Martin Niemoeller in the *Congressional Record*, October 14, 1968, 31636.
21. Liturgy of Baptism in *The Lutheran Book of Worship*, pp. 121-25.

22. Martin Luther, *Small Catechism* in *The Book of Concord*, 360, p. 12.
23. Lutheran biblical authority focuses on "the prophetic and apostolic writings," not on every word in the Bible. *The Book of Concord*, 527, p. 3.
24. Augustine, *Homilies on the Gospel of John*, Tract 24, 1.*Book of Concord*, 220, p. 5.
25. Heinrich Fries and Karl Rahner, *Unity of the Churches: An Actual Possibility*, (Philadelphia: Fortress Press, New York: Paulist Press, 1985), p. 1.
26. H. Richard Niebuhr, *The Kingdom of God in America* (New York: Harper, 1937), p. 193.
27. Billy Sunday in *Jordan's 95 Theses*, Thesis 29.
28. "Hocus-pocus" in *The American Heritage Dictionary of the English Language*, 4th ed. (Boston, 2000).
29. Dietrich Bonhoeffer in Eberhard Bethge, *Dietrich Bonhoeffer: A Biography*, rev. and ed. by Victoria J. Barnett (Minneapolis: Fortress Press, 2000), p. 571.
30. "Eucharist," Second Vatican Council in McGrath, p. 559.
31. "Offertory" in *The Lutheran Book of Worship*, p. 66.
32. *For All the Saints: A Prayer Book For and By the Church*, 4 vols., ed. by Frederick J. Schumacher with Dorothy A. Zelenko (Delhi, NY: ALPB, 1996).
33. Prayer of Alcoholics Anonymous in: Elizabeth Sifton, *The Serenity Prayer* (New York: W. W. Norton, 2003).
34. Martin Luther, "Preface to Georg Rhau's *Symphoniae iucundae*," 1538 in *Luther's Works*, 53, p. 321.
35. "Lift High the Cross" can be found in many hymnals. *Lutheran Book of Worship*, No. 377.
36. "There is a Balm in Gilead" in *With One Voice: A Lutheran Resource for Worship* (Minneapolis: Augsburg Publishing House, 1995), No. 737.
37. *Lutheran Book of Worship*, No. 239.
38. "Mineral," cited with permission from "Crank!" A Record Company, 1223 Wilshire Boulevard #823, Santa Monica, CA 90403.
39. "Eat This Bread" in *With One Voice*, No. 709.